The Blessing Cup

24 Simple Rites for Family Prayer-Celebrations

Rock Travnikar, O.F.M.

Nihil Obstat
Rev. Hilarion Kistner, O.F.M.

Imprimi Potest
Rev. Andrew Fox, O.F.M.
Provincial

Cover, illustrations and book design by Julie Van Leeuwen.

SBN 0-912228-60-1

Table of Contents

Foreword

Who first discovered that rainwater collected in the crease of a leaf or the indentation of a small rock could not only quench an individual's thirst but—a turning point in human development—be shared with another? A telling and poignant beginning in interpersonal relations, to be sure!

And from that lost time, that "accident" in our development, a simple cup has become one of the world's most universal and significant religious symbols. From that natural occurrence where humans shared water to the deep mystery of Eucharist, sharing by cup has symbolized nearly every profound human emotion and divine grace.

By the time religious history was first recorded, and certainly by the time of the Hebrew Scriptures, the cup had become more than a means of serving bodily needs. It had been invested with an unusually persuasive power to convene tribes, to maintain a sensitivity about community, to cause families to remember their roots, and to celebrate God's attention to human needs.

Think of the Old Testament stories in which the cup plays a dramatic role. The beginning of Genesis 44 sets the scene for Joseph to use his treasured divining cup as a means of reconciliation with the envious and conniving brothers who had, years earlier, sold him into Egypt.

Familiar also is the cup of happiness which overflows (Ps 23:5).

The psalms abound with such references: the cup of bitterness, the shepherd's cup, the cup of salvation.

But central to Jewish family life is the cup which brings blessing! Used four times in the lavish and symbolically rich "Seder" during the retelling of the Exodus story, the cup helps families gathered for the meal of Passover know and celebrate who they are in Yahweh, the Lord God.

New Testament usage of the cup is an intense adventure into the dynamics of suffering, compassion, challenge and sacrifice. Once Jesus used the cup to question his followers about their willingness to undergo suffering like his (Mt 20:22). On another occasion, the cup symbolized for Jesus the bitterness he must taste if he would do the Father's will (Mt 26:39).

Eucharist is the high point of Christian sharing of the cup. It is Christ's blood, a true and real presence making the simplest vessel or the most ornate goblet into a sacramental chalice. Just as Eucharist implies joyous thanksgiving shared within the body of Christ, so the cup becomes a symbol for reconciliation within that body.

But what of its ordinary use? How might it serve also in binding together fragmented and pressured families?

Over the past 10 years or more, it has been my delight to witness the "coming of age," so to speak, of this religious symbol in many Christian homes. Many times over these years, I have met with groups of families searching for usable symbols of cohesion or, as one person put it, "a catalyst for causing celebration." The cup is such an instrument if used imaginatively and with sensitivity.

My *Little Liturgies for the Christian Family* (CCS Publishing House, Downers Grove, 1970) and *Celebrations for Special Days and Occasions* (Harper and Row, New York, 1972) were created for families who wish to go beyond the usual routines to bring God and the Christian community into focus in secular experiences such as, for example, birthdays and anniversaries. I tried to provide those who wish to celebrate the spiritual dimension in their homes with some ideas, all centering around the use of the cup of blessing.

Therefore, it is a great delight and pleasure to see how creatively Father Travnikar enriches this family blessing cup devotion through this book. He provides in each service a deep sense of the sacred for Christian families at home.

The list of opportunities for celebrating with a blessing cup is as endless as the variations of family life and times: children making up, anniversaries, Mother's or Father's Day, special holy or religious days, Thanksgiving, when a baby is born or adopted, a homecoming, welcoming new neighbors, First Communion, Confirmation, before entering the hospital, and even on the occasion of a loved pet's death.

Let these times be as festive and relational as the occasion allows. The cup insists upon being passed from one to another. It refuses to become a symbol which stands off by itself, unavailable to the common touch and use. It belongs to our sense of belonging itself!

Cups may be made, found or purchased. In any case, they become a true vehicle of God's grace as we who live in families rehearse our common destiny and dare to share our hopes and fears with those we love.

Jack W. Lundin

Dedication

With gratitude I dedicate this book to my parents, Joseph and Caroline Travnikar. Their example and the blessing they gave me in a home of joyful sons and daughters is the blessing I offer all the families who make the blessing cup a part of their tradition.

Introduction

Every family strives to strengthen its bonds by mutually sharing hopes and fears, joys and sorrows. The blessing cup is a family tradition you can begin in your home to help you toward this goal.

Used as a family symbol, the blessing cup can become a sign of solidarity—oneness in prayer and blessing. The blessing cup service, centered around a common cup and based on the use of Scripture and petition, can help each family member express his or her deepest feelings.

So select a cup—metal, pottery or glass. Keep it in a prominent place to remind you of your mutual hope. Then gather your family for prayer at special times—holidays, birthdays, anniversaries; times of change, growth or loss.

Before beginning your celebration, decide who will lead the prayer and who will read the Scripture. These might be permanent responsibilities; in a growing family it is more likely that roles will become more flexible as the family matures.

Let the filling of the cup be a ceremonious act—even a special privilege—that marks the beginning of a special event. Fill it with your favorite beverage—whatever fits the occasion and the taste of the participants. Then open the prayer with the Sign of the Cross, presenting the significance of the day to the Lord in a few words. Listen together to a brief passage from Scripture that relates to the event you celebrate.

The leader can then announce the response to the petitions and start them with a few prayers formulated in advance. Other family members are then invited to add their own prayers—perhaps a special birthday wish or a particular worry—or left free to pray silently for needs that words refuse to hold.

When the leader senses that all have had their say, he or she collects the family's prayers into one, the "collect," and offers them to the Lord. The unity achieved in prayer is then celebrated by passing the common cup.

A prayer or song lifted in unison, perhaps with hands held around the family circle, seals the individual members as one before the Lord, and the simple ritual is ended.

The family prayer services in this book were inspired by the people of St. Agnes Church in Dayton, Ohio, and the Knightswood and Belle Vista neighborhood groups of St. Therese Church in Fort Wayne, Indiana. It is my hope that these services will be but a springboard to the creative development of your own family's prayer.

May your blessing cup be filled to overflowing!

I.

The Circle of Love

Happy are you who fear the LORD.
  who walk in his ways!
Your wife shall be like a fruitful vine
  in the recesses of your home;
Your children like olive plants
  around your table.
Behold, thus is the man blessed
  who fears the LORD.

Ps 128: 1, 3-4

1. Dedication of the Family Blessing Cup

Opening Prayer

Father, we ask your blessing on us all as we dedicate this cup together, in the name of the Father, and of the Son, and of the Holy Spirit.

Scripture *1 Cor 10:16a*

Is not the cup of blessing we bless a sharing in the blood of Christ?

Petitions

May this cup symbolize our care for each other, Lord, we pray.

Response: Bless us, Lord.

May it represent a shared love which grows by your grace each day, Lord, we pray.

May it be a sign of the trust that we have in you and in each other, Lord, we pray.

May we willingly share our hopes, dreams and fears, our joys and disappointments around our family cup of blessing. Lord, we pray.

Collect

Holy be this cup which we raise in blessing. May we grow in a sense of mutual family love sharing in this one cup.

Sharing of the Blessing Cup

Pray together the Our Father or sing an appropriate song.

2. A Family Prayer

Opening Prayer

We walk together in the light of God's blessing, in the name of the Father, and of the Son, and of the Holy Spirit.

Scripture *Lk 24:35-36*

Then [the disciples] recounted what had happened on the road and how they had come to know him in the breaking of the bread. While they were still speaking about all this, he himself stood in their midst [and said to them, "Peace to you."]

Petitions

May we love one another as Christ loves us, we pray.

Response: We are your family, Lord.

May we grow in our ability to see Christ in each other, we pray.

For the needs of our family and each other, we pray.

Collect

Today, _____ , _____ and _____ have spoken what is in their hearts, recognizing the journey of Christ with this family. May we always walk with Christ.

Sharing of the Blessing Cup

Pray together the Our Father or sing an appropriate song.

3. Prayer for the Blessing of a Home

Opening Prayer

Bless this house, Lord, and those who live here, in the name of the Father, and of the Son, and of the Holy Spirit.

Scripture *Ps 127:1*

Unless the LORD build the house,
  they labor in vain who build it.
Unless the LORD guard the city,
  in vain does the guard keep vigil.

Petitions

We praise and thank you for _____, _____ and _____, who together form this household, as we ask your blessing.

Response: Bless us, Lord.

We pray that this home might be a reflection of the grace-filled home of Nazareth, blessed by Christ himself, as we ask your blessing.

We pray that your Spirit may rest in the hearts of this family and in this home, as we ask your blessing.

Collect

Your abundant goodness has given us cause to rejoice in this people and this place. Send your angels to watch over and to protect all who dwell in this house.

Sharing of the Blessing Cup

Pray together the Our Father or sing an appropriate song.

4. Celebration of Friendship

This service may also be used to welcome new members into the household.

Opening Prayer

Our love for our friends is rooted in Christ Jesus, and so we begin in the name of the Father, and of the Son, and of the Holy Spirit.

Scripture *Jn 14:14-17*

Anything you ask me in my name
I will do.
If you love me
and obey the commands I give you,
I will ask the Father
and he will give you another Paraclete—
to be with you always:
the Spirit of truth.

Petitions

Lord, we thank you for bringing _____ to share in this celebration. Hear us as we pray.

Response: Lord, be with us.

Lord, you made yourself known to a few, yet you are known by many because of your friends. Hear us as we pray.

Lord, give peace and happiness to _____ . Hear us as we pray.

Collect

Blessed are you, Father, for all the works of your goodness, but most especially we thank you for one another in the sharing of this blessing cup. May it be a true sign of friendship.

Sharing of the Blessing Cup

Pray together the Our Father or sing an appropriate song.

5. Celebration of a Birthday

Opening Prayer

We come together to raise our blessing cup and to celebrate the birthday of _____ . We give thanks to God for the life and hope that is within _____ , whose birth we celebrate in the name of the Father, and of the Son, and of the Holy Spirit.

Scripture *Jn 18:37b*

"The reason I was born,
the reason why I came into the world,
is to testify to the truth.
Anyone committed to the truth hears my voice."

Petitions

With thanks to God for revealing Jesus to us through_____ ,
we pray.

Response: Hear us, Lord.

With thanks for the love of Christ which is mirrored in the life of _____ , we pray.

May _____ always be free in the spirit of Christ, we pray.

Collect

Christ, born to redeem humankind, bless us in this celebration.

Sharing of the Blessing Cup

Pray together the Our Father or sing "Happy Birthday" or another appropriate song.

6. Celebration of Family Reconciliation

This service could be used prior to a communal penance service or in the reconciliation of family members.

Opening Prayer

Lord, we have not always been the best sign of your love for us. We are sorry, and we pray in the name of the Father, and of the Son, and of the Holy Spirit.

Scripture *1 Jn 1:9*

If we acknowledge our sins,
he who is just can be trusted
to forgive our sins
and cleanse us from every wrong.

Petitions

Lord, it is you who forgives us. Help us to forgive each other, we pray.

Response: Lord, have mercy.

Lord, we have forgotten your goodness. Help us to return to you, we pray.

Lord, we have failed to remember that everything we are and have is a gift from you. Forgive us, we pray.

Collect

Lord, you have shown us how to live and forgive. For this we are filled with thanks. We will do our best to be new persons, better persons, each day. Help us to be at peace with each other and to forgive in your name.

Sharing of the Blessing Cup

Pray together the Our Father or an act of contrition.

7. In Praise of Nature

Opening Prayer

All seasons give praise to the Creator, and so we pray in the name of the Father, and of the Son, and of the Holy Spirit.

Scripture   *Dt 33:13b-16a*

Blessed by the LORD is his land
   with the best of the skies above
   and of the abyss crouching beneath;
With the best of the produce of the year,
   and the choicest sheaves of the months;
With the finest gifts of the age-old mountains
   and the best from the timeless hills;
With the best of the earth and its fullness.

Petitions

We praise you, Lord, as master of all seasons and times, and we say:

Response: Blessed be God!

We give you thanks for the gift of life, and we say:

In all that you have created we see your glory, and we say:

Collect

Father, we thank you for Jesus, your Son, who lights the darkness of our hearts. Send your Spirit and renew your creation.

Sharing of the Blessing Cup

Pray together the Our Father or sing an appropriate song.

8. Celebration of an Achievement

Opening Prayer

We humbly give thanks for the special strength you have given us in _____ . We celebrate in the name of the Father, and of the Son, and of the Holy Spirit.

Scripture   *2 Tm 4:7*

I have fought the good fight, I have finished the race, I have kept the faith.

Petitions

We pray for _____ on the occasion of _____, and we pray with joy.

Response: Glory to God!

We ask for the courage to accept our failures as well as our accomplishments, and we pray with joy.

We thank our God who is with us in good times and in bad, and we pray with joy.

Collect

We thank you for loving us, Father, so that we could be more than we could ever be alone. We glory in your goodness and praise you in all things.

Sharing of the Blessing Cup

Pray together the Our Father or sing an appropriate song such as "Glory to God, Glory."

9. Prayer in Time of Misfortune or Hardship

Opening Prayer

You know us, Lord, so we turn to you at this time of testing, in the name of the Father, and of the Son, and of the Holy Spirit.

Scripture *2 Cor 4:16-18*

We do not lose heart, because our inner being is renewed each day . . . . The present burden of our trial is light enough, and earns for us an eternal weight of glory beyond all comparison. We do not fix our gaze on what is seen but on what is unseen. What is seen is transitory; what is unseen lasts forever.

Petitions

We ask you to help us in this time of need, especially _____, and we pray.

Response: Be with us, Lord.

Help us to walk by faith, knowing that you will bring good out of every difficulty, we pray.

We thank you for the many gifts you have given to help us through this difficult time, and we pray.

Collect

Lord Jesus, as you lived on this earth you showed us how to deal with trials and hardships. Be with us now. Teach us to trust in you.

Sharing of the Blessing Cup

Pray together the Our Father or sing an appropriate song such as "He's Got the Whole World in His Hands."

10. Prayer at a New Beginning

*This service may also be used to bid farewell to members
leaving the household for a lengthy period of time.*

Opening Prayer

With hope and fear in our hearts we celebrate a new beginning, in the name of the Father, and of the Son, and of the Holy Spirit.

Scripture Nm 6:24-26

"The LORD bless you and keep you!
The LORD let his face shine upon you, and be gracious to you!
The LORD look upon you kindly and give you peace!"

Petitions

Be with _____ as he/she moves in a new direction, Lord, we pray.

Response: You, Lord, are the beginning and the end.

May the sharing and caring of this family be with _____ , Lord, we pray.

In the excitement of a new beginning, guide _____ and calm any anxiety or fears that may arise, Lord, we pray.

Collect

We rejoice in a new beginning which _____ makes today. Guide and keep him/her in your care.

Sharing of the Blessing Cup

Pray together the Our Father or sing an appropriate song such as "Shalom."

11. Prayer When Someone Is Ill

Opening Prayer

In faith we pray for _____, who shares in the suffering of Christ, in the name of the Father, and of the Son, and of the Holy Spirit.

Scripture *Jas 5:13-15a*

If anyone among you is suffering hardship, he must pray. If a person is in good spirits, he should sing a hymn of praise. Is there anyone sick among you? He should ask for the presbyters of the church. They in turn are to pray over him, anointing him with oil in the Name [of the Lord.] This prayer uttered in faith will reclaim the one who is ill, and the Lord will restore him to health.

Petitions

Bless _____ , who is in need of your healing power, we pray, Lord.

Response: Thy will be done.

For doctors, nurses and technicians who share in the healing ministry of Christ, we pray, Lord.

For all the sick and suffering, we pray, Lord.

Collect

God, our Father, send your healing power upon those for whom we pray. We ask this through Jesus Christ, your Son, our Lord.

Sharing of the Blessing Cup

Pray together the Our Father or sing an appropriate song such as "Yahweh Is the God of My Salvation."

12. On the Death of a Loved One

Opening Prayer

Our hearts are heavy as we pray in the name of the Father, and of the Son, and of the Holy Spirit.

Scripture *Jn 11:21-27*

Martha said to Jesus, "Lord, if you had been here, my brother would never have died. Even now, I am sure that God will give you whatever you ask of him." "Your brother will rise again," Jesus assured her. "I know he will rise again," Martha replied, "in the resurrection on the last day." Jesus told her:

"I am the resurrection and the life:
whoever believes in me,
though he should die, will come to life;
and whoever is alive and believes in me
will never die.

Do you believe this?" "Yes, Lord," she replied. "I have come to believe that you are the Messiah, the Son of God: he who is to come into the world."

Petitions

We thank you for the life of _____ , whom you love and whom we love, as we say:

Response: You are the resurrection and the life.

We pray for healing of all the unhappy feelings _____ 's death leaves in our hearts, as we say:

We pray that _____ will share in the glory of your love for all eternity, as we say:

Collect

Be with us, Lord. We trust in you and hope in your glorious Resurrection. We lift up the cup of sorrow, confident that you will change our mourning to rejoicing.

Sharing of the Blessing Cup

Pray together the Our Father or sing an appropriate song such as "I Am the Resurrection and the Life."

II.

Milestones of Christian Life

Know that the LORD is God;
   he made us, his we are;
   his people, the flock he tends.
Enter his gates with thanksgiving,
   his courts with praise;
Give thanks to him; bless his name,
   for he is good:
   the LORD, whose kindness endures forever,
   and his faithfulness, to all generations.

Ps 100: 3-5

13. Celebration of a Baptism

Opening Prayer

We celebrate the rebirth of _____ in the waters of Baptism, in the name of the Father, and of the Son, and of the Holy Spirit.

Scripture *Mk 10:13-16*

People were bringing their little children to him to have him touch them, but the disciples were scolding them for this. Jesus became indignant when he noticed it and said to them: "Let the children come to me and do not hinder them. It is to just such as these that the kingdom of God belongs. I assure you that whoever does not accept the reign of God like a little child shall not take part in it." Then he embraced them and blessed them, placing his hands on them.

Petitions

By the waters of Baptism, bathe _____ in your love, we pray.

Response: Wash us clean, O Lord.

By our celebration of this event renew within us the saving power of our Baptism, we pray.

As members of your family may we together give praise to God our Father, we pray.

Collect

You have made us one by the saving mystery of Baptism. Help us now to be refreshed at the living spring of your goodness in each person.

Sharing of the Blessing Cup

Pray together the Our Father or sing an appropriate song such as "Rejoice in the Lord Always."

14. In Honor of
a First Communion

Opening Prayer

Today we celebrate the wonderful promise of the Last Supper, in the name of the Father, and of the Son, and of the Holy Spirit.

Scripture *Mt 26:26-28*

During the meal Jesus took bread, blessed it, broke it, and gave it to his disciples. "Take this and eat it," he said, "this is my body." Then he took a cup, gave thanks, and gave it to them. "All of you must drink from it," he said, "for this is my blood, the blood of the covenant, to be poured out in behalf of many for the forgiveness of sin."

Petitions

We are grateful for the bread of life you give us. With joy, we pray.

Response: Lord Jesus, you are the bread of life.

We thank you and praise you for _____ 's First Communion which we celebrate. With joy, we pray.

May we all be one at your eternal banquet forever. With joy, we pray.

Collect

Father, we thank you for the wonderful gift of your unconditional love for us. May we grow closer to you and to each other in the sacrament of the Eucharist.

Sharing of the Blessing Cup

Pray together the Our Father or sing an appropriate song.

15. In Preparation for Confirmation

Opening Prayer

With the hopeful promise of your guidance, we pray in the name of the Father, and of the Son and of the Holy Spirit.

Scripture *Acts 2:1-4*

When the day of Pentecost came it found them gathered in one place. Suddenly from up in the sky there came a noise like a strong, driving wind which was heard all through the house where they were seated. Tongues as of fire appeared, which parted and came to rest on each of them. All were filled with the Holy Spirit. They began to express themselves in foreign tongues and made bold proclamation as the Spirit prompted them.

Petitions

We pray that _____ will be filled with the grace and power of your Spirit. Hear our prayer, Lord.

Response: Send your Spirit, Lord.

We pray that all of us will be living examples of Christ's life for each other. Hear our prayer, Lord.

We pray that _____ may joyfully serve the Church. Hear our prayer, Lord.

Collect

Lord, complete the calling you gave us at Baptism. In the power of your Spirit let us proclaim your goodness to the ends of the earth.

Sharing of the Blessing Cup

Pray together the Our Father or sing an appropriate song such as "Come, Holy Ghost."

16. For Vocations to Ministry in the Church

Opening Prayer

In every age leaders are called from the community to proclaim the message of Jesus. For the needs of our own age we pray, in the name of the Father, and of the Son, and of the Holy Spirit.

Scripture *Mt 10:5a, 7-8*

Jesus sent these men on mission as the Twelve, after giving them the following instructions: " . . . As you go, make this announcement: 'The reign of God is at hand!' Cure the sick, raise the dead, heal the leprous, expel demons. The gift you have received, give as a gift."

Petitions

That priests, brothers and sisters will grow in the spirit of Christ Jesus, we pray.

Response: Send laborers into the harvest, Lord.

For those who serve our parish in lay ministry, we pray.

That men and women everywhere will hear God's call to them and find the grace and the courage to answer, we pray.

Collect

Lord, we recommit ourselves to serving the Church with hope and enthusiasm. Help us to recognize the needs of our faith community and to serve it better.

Sharing of the Blessing Cup

Pray together the Our Father or sing an appropriate song such as "Of My Hands."

17. In Honor of Marriage

This service may be used to celebrate a wedding or an anniversary.

Opening Prayer

Father, we commemorate with joy your presence in our life. In that spirit we celebrate the gift of your sacrament of marriage, in the name of the Father, and of the Son, and of the Holy Spirit.

Scripture *Ru 1:16-17a*

"Do not ask me to abandon or forsake you! for wherever you go I will go, wherever you lodge I will lodge, your people shall be my people, and your God my God. Wherever you die I will die, and there be buried."

Petitions

Lord, you blessed the marriage feast at Cana; now bless _____ and _____ , we pray.

Response; Keep us in your love, Lord.

Let the love they have for each other be a faithful reflection of your love, we pray.

Bless all called to share in this sacrament with an abundance of your goodness, we pray.

Collect

We raise the cup of blessing to celebrate the promise of love man and woman make before God. May the covenant of love we celebrate today bring us to eternal life in your love.

Sharing of the Blessing Cup

Pray together the Our Father or sing an appropriate song.

18. On the Occasion or Jubilee of Religious Vows or Ordination

Opening Prayer

We praise and thank you in your servant ＿＿＿＿ for the wonderful gifts you bestow on your people, in the name of the Father, and of the Son, and of the Holy Spirit.

Scripture Ps 116:12-18

How shall I make a return to the LORD
   for all the good he has done for me?
The cup of salvation I will take up,
   and I will call upon the name of the LORD
My vows to the LORD I will pay
   in the presence of all his people.
Precious in the eyes of the LORD
   is the death of his faithful ones.
O LORD, I am your servant;
   I am your servant, the son of your handmaid;
   you have loosed my bonds.
To you will I offer sacrifice of thanksgiving,
   and I will call upon the name of the LORD.
My vows to the LORD I will pay
   In the presence of all his people.

Petitions

Father in heaven, we ask your blessing on ＿＿＿＿ , your servant, as we pray.

Response: Lord, be with your servant.

We rejoice in the gift of Spirit which fills ＿＿＿＿ , as we pray.

May your people be willing to hear the good news proclaimed by ＿＿＿＿, we pray.

Collect

A joyful cup of celebration we raise in honor of ＿＿＿＿ . You,

Lord, are the eternal shepherd who inspires those who lead the Christian community. We give praise and rejoice.

Sharing of the Blessing Cup

Pray together the Our Father or sing an appropriate song.

III.

Seasons and Holidays

You have crowned the year with your bounty,
    and your paths overflow with a rich harvest;
The untilled meadows overflow with it,
    and rejoicing clothes the hills.
The fields are garmented with flocks
    and the valleys blanketed with grain.
    They shout and sing for joy.

Ps 65: 12-14

---

19. Advent Service

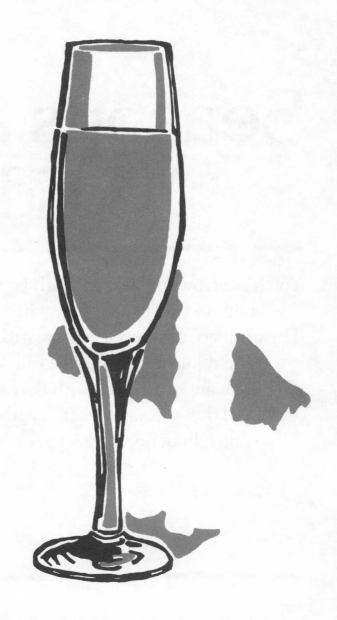

Opening Prayer

As we seek to prepare for the coming of the Lord, we pray in the name of the Father, and of the Son, and of the Holy Spirit.

Scripture *Mt 1:18-21*

Now this is how the birth of Jesus Christ came about. When his mother Mary was engaged to Joseph, but before they lived together, she was found with child through the power of the Holy Spirit. Joseph her husband, an upright man unwilling to expose her to the law, decided to divorce her quietly. Such was his intention when suddenly an angel of the Lord appeared in a dream and said to him: "Joseph, son of David, have no fear about taking Mary as your wife. It is by the Holy Spirit that she has conceived this child. She is to have a son and you are to name him Jesus because he will save his people from their sins."

Petitions

Help us to make room in our hearts for you, Lord, we pray.

Response: We wait for you, Lord.

Help us to proclaim your coming, Lord, we pray.

Help us to live in your love, Lord, we pray.

Collect

Lord, help us to step out in faith and openness to your will. Make us ready to greet you with peace-filled hearts.

Sharing of the Blessing Cup

Pray together the Our Father or sing an Advent song.

20. Christmas Celebration

Opening Prayer

We celebrate the birth of Jesus, in the name of the Father, and of the Son, and of the Holy Spirit.

Scripture *Lk 2:10a, 11-14*

The angel said to [the shepherds]: "This day in David's city a savior has been born to you, the Messiah and Lord. Let this be a sign to you: in a manger you will find an infant wrapped in swaddling clothes." Suddenly, there was with the angel a multitude of the heavenly host, praising God and saying,
   "Glory to God in high heaven,
      peace on earth to those on whom his favor rests."

Petitions

We celebrate the great gift of God's Son, Jesus himself, and we pray.

Response: Glory to God in the highest!

May our family become more and more like the Holy Family, we pray.

May peace fill our hearts, our home and our world, we pray.

Collect

May the happiness of this day bring new hope to the year ahead and joy to our hearts today.

Sharing of the Blessing Cup

Pray together the Our Father or the Hail Mary, or sing your favorite Christmas hymn.

21. Lenten Service

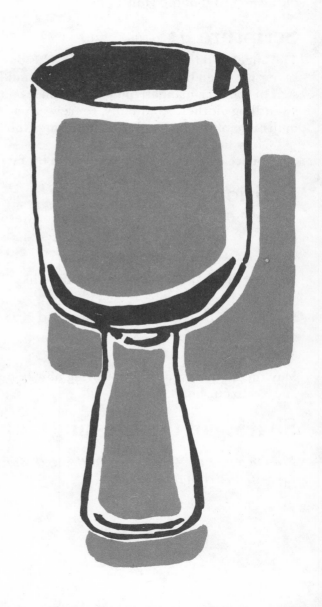

Opening Prayer

Lent reminds us to pray and to do penance, and so we begin in the name of the Father, and of the Son, and of the Holy Spirit.

Scripture *Mt 4:1-2*

Then Jesus was led into the desert by the Spirit to be tempted by the devil. He fasted forty days and forty nights, and afterwards was hungry.

Petitions

Change our hearts and renew our love for you, Lord, we pray.

Response: Be with us, Lord.

Help us to bring order into our lives so that others may find you there, Lord, we pray.

By sharing your suffering may we also come to rejoice in your Resurrection, Lord, we pray.

Collect

Lord, be with us as we look forward to new birth at Easter. Let us shine forth with the joy of your rising.

Sharing of the Blessing Cup

Pray together the Our Father or sing an appropriate Lenten hymn.

22. Easter Celebration

Opening Prayer

The Lord is risen, alleluia! Let us celebrate in the name of the Father, and of the Son, and of the Holy Spirit.

Scripture *Lk 24:3-8*

When [the women] entered the tomb, they did not find the body of the Lord Jesus. While they were still at a loss over what to think of this, two men in dazzling garments stood beside them. Terrified, the women bowed to the ground. The men said to them: "Why do you search for the Living One among the dead? He is not here; he has been raised up. Remember what he said to you while he was still in Galilee—that the Son of Man must be delivered into the hands of sinful men, and be crucified, and on the third day rise again." With this reminder, his words came back to them.

Petitions

In his rising from the dead, Jesus has given us the power of rising above ourselves; may we walk in the light which brightens the path of faith, we pray.

Response: Alleluia!

May the Lord be with us as he was with the faithful on that first Easter, we pray.

May this cup be a sign of joy—the joy of Christians renewed by Christ's rising, we pray.

Collect

Help us, Lord, to rise above ourselves. Break our hearts of stone so that we truly may shine as children of light and life.

Sharing of the Blessing Cup

Pray together the Our Father or sing an appropriate Easter song.

23. Mother's or Father's Day

Opening Prayer

The first of all teachers are our parents. We pray for them in a special way this day as we pray in the name of the Father, and of the Son, and of the Holy Spirit.

Scripture *Eph 3:14-16a*

That is why I kneel before the Father from whom every family in heaven and on earth takes its name; and I pray that he will bestow on you gifts in keeping with the riches of his glory.

Petitions

Grant your blessing to our Mother/Father on this special day which honors her/him.

Response: Bless our Mother/Father, Lord.

Keep us in your care so that we might live in the pattern of the Holy Family, we pray.

For those who have not been blessed with the love that fills our home, we pray.

Collect

Lord, we thank you for allowing us to celebrate this special day. May we continue to live the lessons we have learned from our parents.

Sharing of the Blessing Cup

Pray together the Our Father or Hail Mary, or sing an appropriate song.

24. Thanksgiving Day

Opening Prayer

In the spirit of humble praise we give thanks, in the name of the Father, and of the Son, and of the Holy Spirit.

Scripture *Ps 106:1-2*

Give thanks to the Lord, for he is good,
 for his kindness endures forever.
Who can tell the mighty deeds of the Lord,
 or proclaim all his praises?

Petitions

For our family, friends, relatives and those who teach us of God's way, we pray.

Response: We thank you, Lord.

For our home and for the many things you surround us with in goodness, we pray.

For all creation, for sights and sounds and all our senses, we pray.

Collect

We lift up this cup to our God with gratitude for all he does for his people.

Sharing of the Blessing Cup

Join hands and pray together the Our Father.